Christma

G000094342

Ten Poems to Wa

ex libris

Candlestick Press

Published by:
Candlestick Press,
Diversity House, 72 Nottingham Road, Arnold, Nottingham NG5 6LF
www.candlestickpress.co.uk

Design and typesetting by Craig Twigg

Printed by Ratcliff & Roper Print Group, Nottinghamshire, UK

Cover illustration © Louise Slater, 2019
www.louiseslater.com

Candlestick Press monogram © Barbara Shaw, 2008

© Candlestick Press, 2019

ISBN 978 1 907598 83 8

Acknowledgements:

Thanks are due to all the copyright holders cited below for their kind permission:

Fleur Adcock, poem as yet unpublished, by kind permission of the author

Jo Brandon, poem as yet unpublished, by kind permission of the author

Martin Figura, poem as yet unpublished, by kind permission of the author

Seán Hewitt, poem as yet unpublished, by kind permission of the author

Phil Houghton, poem as yet unpublished, by kind permission of the author

Rosie Jackson, poem as yet unpublished, by kind permission of the author

L Kiew, poem as yet unpublished, by kind permission of the author

Theophilus Kwek, poem as yet unpublished, by kind permission of the author

Katrina Porteous, poem as yet unpublished, by kind permission of the author

James Sheard, poem as yet unpublished, by kind permission of the author

Contents   Page

The Golden Bough

handed to guardians of the underworld was mistletoe,
garlands plucked for luck to keep shadows at bay;
soldiers in the First World War had sprigs sewn onto cards,
hopeful amulets. *Mystyldene. Devil's fuge. All-heal.*

But the legend I like most is of Frigga, Norse goddess
of love, queen of *seidr* - magic - who could summon events
into being, robe herself with falcon plumes, turn into a bird.
Yet when her son, Balder, was killed by an arrow

crafted from mistletoe, she could not save him, but wept
and wept – what mother would not grieve her lost child?
– wept over the fatal twig until her tears formed into pearls,
lucent emblems of her unstoppable love.

I think of her when I walk in parkland in winter, where poplars
foster baubles of mistletoe, perfect spheres cradled against
an impassive sky. I think of my own son, many losses,
and the different endings of Frigga's story: how some say

Balder was never restored to life and the world was plunged
into endless darkness; others, that the gods repented when they saw
his mother's sorrow, and she stood in a delirium of gratitude
under the mistletoe, happy to kiss anyone who passed.

I stand here now in the bleak light as she must have done then,
back pressed against bark – apple, hawthorn, lime – looking up
at the stark lattice of branches, their bunches of mistletoe harboured
like refugee moons. And I want to cry out, as Frigga did,

to the air and birds and new-found tenderness of the world
that love is surely bigger than grief, than death.
Come, stand with me beneath these white berries of love.
Let me hold you, kiss you.

Rosie Jackson

- 5 -

Tannenbaum

My first job was a long day
in the village – fifteen, and I worked
each December through the bite
of the wind hauling trees, unsheathing

the smell of them, carols
between the static of the radio
and the smell of the pine
thick in my clothes, heat

of work and column of breath
in the steeling light. How
the stars would prick
through the cold sky early on, white

on blue, the streets frozen
and emptying. And one night
I would bring our tree home, shake it
from the netting, all of us

chattering, cross-legged,
untangling the lights, a new
constellation on the branches,
the angel's trumpet flourish,

and the top of the tree bent
like a gilt crozier. I remember
long into the evening,
the songs lifting, crack of the fire –

and outside a rare silence,
where even the clap of a voice
might make the snow
slide its body from the eaves.

Seán Hewitt

Choirboys

They would appear during Advent, floating up
from the battered tins of special paint, stored
in the tin trunk with the decorations.

Bold, abstract, reds and gold, the white of their cassocks –
the windows of every house we lodged in
would be painted with robed and singing choirboys.

It was my Mum's one arty skill, I used to think, learnt
at college, or perhaps at those early schools she taught in:
the one with one schoolroom and the earth middens;

or the one where the rougher kids clog-clumped across the floors,
tormented the class tortoise, killed the goldfish, then
disappeared for days at lambing and at harvest.

We lived abroad. And so the light beyond the window
might be the bulbous greys of the Northeast Monsoon;
the brilliance of the Eastern Med, bright off the sea;

or the bounce and glare of Westphalia under early snow.
However it had reached us, this was our tradition –
a mock-staining of glass for the sun to touch off

the imagined sound of carols, sung badly, loudly,
soaring upwards in a church back in England somewhere.

James Sheard

This year like last year

Christmas is out on the village green,
the church choir singing carols is a woolly hat
all warm and soft around my head.
Everyone smells of the mulled wine
that's only 50p a mug, I like the mizzle-blur
of fairy lights against the dark, Santa sitting sleigh-high,
his beard so bouncy and white, it hides his red chest.
Does anybody else know that Santa
is a robin?

His reindeer are resting somewhere quiet,
their bellies rumbling for carrots,
we cut ours into sticks so they can eat them quicker.
Waiting to meet Santa, we shuffle and stomp,
chatter and fidget in the cold, my scarf itches,
my glove has a hole in the thumb, it hasn't snowed
yet, he double-checks we've been good,
he looks a little different to last year
so do you, Mum says.
Do you remember me, Father Christmas?

Walking back home clutching our gifts,
we see Christmas through other people's windows,
Dad comments on the decoration of their trees,
his goodwill needs to warm up by the fire,
I shouldn't sit too close to the grate or I'll turn
into Rudolph's nose.

I like that Christmas is always the same, someone
on the telly said, 'the best days are always short' –
it could have been the Vicar of Dibley,
or the Queen.

Jo Brandon

Seniors' Activity Corner
Christmas Eve, Singapore

Late-night TV mimes on-screen, while rain
pools unnoticed in the lumpy grass. I'm
out again, sleepless, when I see them
on a long thin bench holding court, minding

their own business. *Nothing's changed,* says
Melchior, slapping the stone table
so as to get the last word, though Caspar
isn't letting him have it. *Naw, it's always*

the same with you, gloomy git! (And
here Balthazar chimes in,) *world hasn't*
quite ended yet, has it? Round and round
they go, these three – kings of all there is –

as doors shut, the children climb to their beds,
and further yet, a lone star rises, sets.

Theophilus Kwek

Promise

There is a light
at the Year's edge
the twitching gap
in the curtains
eager
but, finding it still
dark
it is a glimmer
at the edge
of humanity
lamp-lighting
the who-we-are's
and who-we-might-be's
it is the moon slit
cut
into winter-dark clouds
illuminating
the star-handed,
pressed-to-the-pane
impatience
of children
waiting
still
but more so, the sunburst
glow
of a kind act
warm tea
handed
pavement-side
reflecting
growing smiles
hands
unwrapping
its real meaning
                    when there was no room
in the coming
Light

Phil Houghton

Christmas Lights

Christmas begins, as always in this house
with a prod and the hatch dropping open
with an astonished gasp, a firmament
of dust sudden in the naked light.

We don't need to witness it, to believe
in our father's careful ascension
of the loft ladder, his white hair
the corona to an eclipse as he enters

the chaos of the void. Blown fuses
are the biggest culprits of broken
Christmas lights. Electrical cables
pass through each other like ghosts

when unobserved. All bulbs are equal
in the eyes of resistance tests. Somewhere
along the continuum exists the end
of the Sellotape. Railway timetables

are little more than symbolic. Over time
connections may become corroded
with grime. By some miracle all of us
have made it and the good news is

the evangelists are singing a capella
in the dim underpass. The cul-de-sac
is visible from outer space; father laments
the advent of such crass gimcrackery,

holds that home is a flickering bulb, true
spirit, the low illumination of coloured
plastic, has a pair of long-nose pliers
and enough spare bulbs to *see him out.*

Martin Figura

December began with shopping

for the exotic: mint and apple sauce,
imported rosemary, cranberries, candied
peel and blocks of English butter.

It began with baking, the Christmas cake
drenched daily with dark brandy
until it oozed from the lightest finger-flick

and emptying jar after jar
of Robertson's mincemeat into pastry.
Cinnamon gold-dusted everything.

After the final Advent window,
we opened all our doors,
welcoming hungry occupants, their cars

filling up the driveway, aunts and uncles,
cousins in greater and lesser iterations,
the generations dressed in batik, bearing gifts.

The kitchen was ever at the heart of it.
My parents cooked together.
Crackling, perfection an inch thick

on the side of pig that Dad roasted
while Mum beatified the oven-pan,
red wine gravy, bliss of roux.

Cheerful, family sat where we could,
plates heavy in heady heat, heaped
meat, golden potatoes, peas, carrots too.

Our hands were full. Still there was more,
glasses, cups, Anchor beer and Sunkist,
hot kopi, Cointreau, joyful chatter,

mince pies with cream, walnuts
to crack and chocolates to unwrap.
Dad asked again, again and

again if we'd enough to eat
until decidedly replete, my extended family
levered to their feet, departed noisily.

Day cooled to a close. Dusk drifted quiet
through rooms to settle on stacks
of washing up glinting in the sink.

It was always good, that stillness,
sky kissed with flecks of light,
night unbuttoning its mysteries.

L Kiew

The Other Christmas Poem

Or you might prefer to read about the Christmas
when after all the hosting and feasting

we finally got the kids off to bed
and the rest of us, the grown-ups
(if that's an accurate designation),

opened up another case of wine
and put on some Rolling Stones records.

I think it was Ruth, a friend of a friend,
who found the room a bit overheated
and made the decision to take her top off –

something it seemed she was given to doing
at the slightest provocation.

Her husband greeted this with tolerance,
and before too long had removed his shirt;
several other people shed theirs.

One of the women undid her dress,
with a vaguely absent-minded air.

The dancing hotted up; Ruth took off her bra;
someone stepped casually out of his trousers.
You can see the way this is going.

By the time Alex tiptoed upstairs
for more wine from the stash in his study

(the children, thank God, were sleeping soundly)
he was the only adult in the house
wearing so much as his underpants.

Ah, what a memorable party,
we'd reminisce in the years that followed,

thinking of the camaraderie –
and of how our necks had been stiff with the strain
of never glancing below anyone's waist.

Fleur Adcock

The Mizzletow

This is the night the world turns upside down,
I tell the excited children, awaiting delivery
Of a sack-load of chocolate and electronics. There was an old man

I remember, remembered the Guizers, masks on their faces,
Carrying besoms and a fragment of an old play –
St George and a fight to the death and a doctor – *'Gliffin' the horses,*

Scarin' us bairns and the aa'd uns, hammerin' like hell
On the doors, cowpin' the rainwatter barrels.' Bringing havoc –
For this was the same and a different country, I tell them,

No cards, no tree, no Santa. A colder, greener,
Pitiless country, far from the town, roots clenched under snow,
The hinds' raa's and fisher squares fending off hunger

Until this night. This rammage. Then the Yule Doo,
Sweetened with sticky currants, the frummerty steaming,
And a burning cold dragged in from the dark – the Mizzletow –

Strange, aromatic. A tang of field edges. *Mizzle,* a thin rain –
Not the pearly southern berries, but hoops of bitter willow
Wound into a globe with the ivy and evergreen

Of the inside-out world. Then, fervent with something so deep
He had set it aside and never gone back, the old man would falter.
But the children are not listening. They are asleep.

Katrina Porteous

Northumberland in the early 20th century retained many ancient traditions. The
language was heavily Anglo Saxon, with earlier and later elements. Guizers are
mummers, besoms are brooms, to gliff is to scare and to cowp is to overturn. Hinds' raa's
were farm labourers' cottages. A rammage is a rampage, Yule Doo are pastry effigies,
and frummerty is boiled barley. The Mizzletow was an elaborate Christmas wreath,
wound into a sphere of willow and evergreen.